LEARNING TO PITCH SOFTBALL

3rd Edition

2019

By Jim Webb

"Coach Webb" grew up playing fastpitch softball, and continued in ASA men's fastpitch competition, winning more than 600 games as a pitcher over 24 years. His own strikeout records are 29 in a fourteen inning game, 18 in a seven inning game, and 14 in a five inning game. He pitched 45 no-hitters and 6 perfect games. Two of his three college degrees were in physical education and included the study of biomechanics and kinesiology. Having given lessons for more than 30 years to more than 10,000 girls, more than 200 of his students have won national championships. He has been the featured speaker and clinician at dozens of national and state coaching meetings. In college coaching he has produced more than two dozen All-American pitchers and has worked with the coaches and players of the national teams of ten countries.

TABLE OF CONTENTS

INTRODUCTION

Many things about pitching border on controversial, and some areas cannot be defined clearly as right or wrong, and what is effective often varies from pitcher to pitcher. Also, the rules enforcement and interpretations are different at the different levels and locations, and many rules have changed over the years and will continue to change. In this book I tell my point of view and what I have learned from my own pitching and from teaching thirty years of lessons; and also, from my education and study of biomechanics. I hope you will find something useful to continue your learning and teaching effectively. It contains teaching strategy and reasoning, mechanics identification, the correction of mistakes, tips on control, speed and movement, and the cause and effect of certain mechanics.

CHAPTER 1 – In the Beginning

This is the opportunity for the coach to pass along his/her love of the game. It is the opportunity to have a positive impact on the future of the game which is in the hands of our young players. Participation, especially at the beginning levels, should have several goals. One is to teach the fundamental understanding and skills of the game, and one is to teach teamwork. There are many more, but probably the most important of all for beginners is that they enjoy the game and have fun in it. If it is too serious or too stressful at the beginning, they will drop out before they have a chance to learn and develop. Having fun does not mean throwing away the rules, or placing no importance on winning, or laughing at mistakes. It means sharing with compassion all the processes and outcomes and being able to place this activity in a proper and meaningful perspective. It also means learning respect for the game, the coaches, and the participants. To accomplish this, there must be positive feedback and rewards for effort, achievement and sportsmanship. At times pitching can be a frustrating skill for both the player and coach. Practice and learning must be made into a rewarding and enjoyable experience.

"Who Should Pitch?"

One of the more common questions I have been asked is how to choose the player to pitch. What is important in the selection of the player for this position? There is a long list of positive factors that can cause someone to become a good pitcher. Every coach would probably first choose the player who is tall or strong looking. But I have found that the single most important factor in choosing a pitcher is "How badly does that player want to pitch?" The ones who want to do it the most will go through difficulties and will practice the most. They will place a level of importance, dedication, focus and discipline on pitching that may never be felt by most of the team. A good pitcher can develop from any size or shape. For someone who really wants to be a pitcher, it is fairly easy to focus on becoming the best she can be. Probably the easiest way to answer the question of "how much does a player want to pitch" is to find out "how much does a player want to practice?" A quality that will be an advantage for a young pitcher is "being stubborn." Someone who will not give up easily when the chips are down will eventually become successful.

"Advice for a parent"

Buy your child a "softie" ball, which has the same size, weight, seams and feel as the game ball, and get yourself a first baseman's glove and find a five-gallon bucket to sit on. The softie ball will save you broken shins and ribs and help you enjoy catching more if you are not worried about personal injury to yourself. The softie balls are available in both 12" and 11" sizes. If your daughter is fast or wild, you may also need to get some catching gear. A first-baseman's glove is easier to catch with than a catcher's glove, especially if the pitcher is a little wild. The bucket is lower than a folding chair and makes you a better target for your pitcher. Make or buy a throw-down home plate from something as thin as possible (like a towel), not something with a lip which will cause a bad hop if the pitched ball hits the front edge of it. If you have a block wall or a backstop available, you can also hang or tape a bath towel or pillowcase to it which is the approximate size of the strike zone.

It is important for parents to take their daughter to pitching clinics or to lessons and to give her contact with people that will cause her development and be motivational to her. It is also important to teach her the importance of warming up correctly, stretching and general conditioning, and then icing when practice or the game is over. At the beginning level, the coaches may be volunteers and not have the time or knowledge or resources to do these things.

"Control or Speed"

At the youngest age level, control is taken out of the picture by using a tee, then a pitching machine, and then by having coach-pitch. At the beginning level of competitive play with a pitcher, the pitcher that throws the most strikes will almost always win. Since winning is very important, some coaches will sacrifice mechanics and speed

Coach Webb catching a lesson

to get the pitcher to throw strikes. However, within the next few years the scenario changes, and the pitcher who throws the fastest will begin to win all the games. It continues to evolve during the age development to the one with the most movement; and then finally to the one who can do all these.

When asked which is most important, speed or control, I compare it to running the 100 meter dash. Is it most important to cross the finish line first or to stay in your running lane? Both speed and control are most important. The only way to learn the control of speed is to throw fast all the time. Actually the mechanics which cause speed also cause good control. The next chapters will deal with issues which cause or detract from speed and control.

"When to begin movement pitches"

At any age, when a pitcher has good command of her mechanics and maximum velocity, it is possible to start working on ball spins. When young or when the hands are very small, she may not be able to throw these pitches with power, but it will still begin the process of building muscle memory of the releases. I have had many ten and eleven-year-old students who were able to throw perfect spins for the rise, drop and curve. This is not like throwing the curve with a baseball. First of all, the baseball is heavier than the softball, and second the angles and flexion of the wrist for different pitches are different from baseball, and third the distance the ball is thrown is shorter. If a young pitcher learns to throw the spins, she will be able to master the pitches much more quickly when her physical growth catches up with her knowledge.

CHAPTER 2 – Components of Speed

Maximum speed is a result of a combination of (1) the principles and mechanics of force application and power transfer, and (2) the absence of mechanical and physical flaws which would deter from force transfer. The goal is to achieve the positive components and eliminate the negative components in the pitch delivery.

"Arm speed" is the most obvious component of ball speed. For the arm to go around the circle fast, it should be in one plane. There are a number of factors that allow it. The arm should be straight and not rotate along its long axis during the arm circle. Turning the hand back in the upper back of the circle will slow the arm speed and cause a hitch in the circle. The wrist and elbow should not be locked or rigid but should be relaxed and straight to form the longest power lever possible.

When the plane of the arm circle is in line with the plate, the fastest and smoothest circle can be made when the shoulders and hips turn 40-60 degrees. This turn should happen approximately when the pitching hand is in the front of the circle pointed toward the plate. In the front of the arm circle both the glove hand and ball hand will be pointed forward with the glove hand nearer the plate. If the shoulders rotate too far, it will cause the circle to get out of the plane of flight and the hand will get too far behind the back. This sometimes happens when the pitcher rotates the pivot foot and "squashes the bug" causing the shoulder turn to be generated from the feet rather than from the arms.

The fastest arm speed during the release of the ball can be achieved if the pitching side shoulder is not turning or closing during the release. Closing the pitching side shoulder during the release is a slow movement compared to the hand speed and will slow the hand down if the upper arm clamps to the ribs at the release point. If the shoulder closes ahead of the release, it puts dangerous torque on the rotator cuff and also causes a control problem. With the pitching shoulder slightly turned, the palm of the hand can face any of the directions required for any of the pitch releases. However, when the shoulder closes to the plate, the palm can no longer stay in the position required for several of the spins.

Another problem which takes away speed is bending the elbow before or during the release. First, it shortens the lever before the power is applied to the ball. Second, it changes where the palm and fingers point, so it eliminates the possibility of correct spin for several of the pitches. Third, it shortens the area where a ball may be released and still throw a strike. It tends to transfer the arm force into the ball upward rather than in the direction of the plate. It is not necessary to intentionally flex the elbow during the follow through, as it is wasted energy and happens after the ball is gone. The follow through should be a natural and relaxed motion that is the result of the power and speed of the release and of the spinning of the particular pitch. Exaggerating the follow through will often make the release late and cause the pitcher to throw high and lose the desired spin.

"Wrist snap" The importance of this flexing of the wrist is sometimes overdone. Its purpose is a relaxed whippy, slinging, rolling off the fingers action. The wrist should be relaxed rather than a muscular jerk-stop movement. The weight of the ball and the centrifugal force of the arm circle will cause this flexion to happen if the wrist is relaxed. The release from the fingers will obviously be different for the different pitches, so the speeds of the pitches will not all be the same. The ability to relax the wrist and arm will be a major factor in the ability to achieve spin speed in each of the pitches. When the arm goes around the circle and the shoulder rotates properly, the hand and wrist will keep their correct position for a good

Wrist snap – Jessica Leenerts

wrist snap. It is not necessary to turn the
palm back in the upper back of the circle.

Doing that slows the arm speed and has to be unlearned when learning hand position for the different pitches. The wrist snap causes an acceleration from the arm speed when applied during the release (like the end of a whip). That causes the ball speed to accelerate on the way to the plate, and in the case of movement pitches, makes the movement more sudden.

Feet and Legs: The feet are responsible for balance, posture, and timing. The legs are responsible for power. With a pitcher who uses the mechanics to throw with arms, the adjustments of using the feet and legs correctly can add up to 5 mph to her pitch speed. A fairly experienced pitcher may throw 60 mph just using the arms and has already accumulated 10 million pitches of muscle memory to the way she throws the ball. It is not easy or quick to overcome this. It is surprising how many pitchers squash the bug with the pivot foot, or pitch with both knees locked, or move their center of gravity forward only in the front half of the arm circle, or leap and land before the hand is to the top of the arm circle. Doing these things uses needless big energy and puts body parts in jeopardy to injury. Correct balance, posture, and timing will not only maximize speed but will contribute to endurance, durability, control, and movement.

In the preliminary stance, the feet should be enough apart to have a comfortable foundation, and far enough apart to transfer the weight from the stride foot to the pivot foot as the pitching motion begins. The stride toe is touching the back of the pitching rubber, pointed toward the plate. The pivot toe is to be over the front edge of the pitching rubber, pointed slightly toward the pitching side of the plate. When a base runner takes a position on the base to lead off and steal, the ankle action of that push off foot is the same as what the pivot foot should do in the initial push. If in the first movements of the arms, the pivot foot toe and knee turn out, then the pitcher has just lost a major component of power and will probably also turn the shoulder and hips too far and lose arm speed when the result is getting the ball behind the back.

From the stance, the preliminary move of the feet and legs should be to shift the weight from the stride foot to the pivot foot and then bend the pivot knee and push away and stride with the pivot foot. The inside of the toe or foot should drag forward and not cross over to the opposite side, because it would pull the pitching shoulder back during the release. It also causes the pitcher to land and fall back, not keeping good posture during the release.

The stride foot should be in a straight line to the landing spot. Often a pitcher who squashes the bug will start the stride foot across and then pull it back to the stride side to land. That adversely affects the angle of the hips and shoulders during the release. Stepping across the midline will also put huge torque on the lower back. In the production of force, it is like a pair of scissors with the lines of force production going sideways to either or both sides of the plate rather than all forces straight to the target. I have actually seen some pitchers end the pitch with their arms crossed from doing this. With practice the pitcher may train to change where she lands with the stride foot for achieving the desired location of the pitch.

The foot should not land with the toe pointed at a 90 degree (or more) angle to the line of the ball flight. It not only affects the control but also is really hard on the knee and ankle and will eventually be the cause of injury.

Balance/Posture – Becky Duffin

The knee of the stride foot should be not locked but straight and stable at the landing. Any flexing of this knee during landing will adversely affect both speed and control. On the change-up it also tips off the pitch to the batter. A pitcher that bends the front knee in landing will have an inconsistent point of release and will continually have trouble with high and low control. The posture for throwing speed should be upright and balanced, the same as in walking and running. Leaning forward or back will take away power and cause other mechanical results.

Timing: I have described what each foot and knee should do, but the big key to this is when it is done. The timing relationship of "the arm circle and release" to "the push away, the stride and landing" are what cause the most efficient and powerful application of force.

The biggest muscles in the body are in the legs. We want to take advantage of this, and cause power to come from the legs. I have seen pitchers stride or jump completely out of the pitching circle, but they landed before their arm got to 11 o'clock in the arm circle, and the forward movement of their center of gravity all happened between 6 o'clock and 10 o'clock in the front half of their arm circle. What I want to teach is that the arm motion should be ahead of the legs, so that the production of the legs is happening in the back half of the arm circle from 1 o'clock to 5 o'clock. From 5 o'clock to 7 o'clock is the wrist snap "cracking of the whip" through the release.

Starting the arm circle while shifting the weight from the stride foot to the pivot foot will allow the pitching arm to get further out before the stride foot steps forward (getting the arm ahead of the foot.) Shifting the weight as the preliminary arm motion happens, also delays or prolongs the moving forward of the center of gravity to the back of the arm circle. The power and acceleration phase of the arm circle is from 4 o'clock to 7 o'clock. Ideally the center of gravity can still be moving forward to the first part of this phase of the arm circle. A measurement or checkpoint of this timing is to see where the pitching hand is when the stride foot comes off the ground (7 to 8 o'clock is good); where the pitching hand is when the pivot foot leaves the rubber (11 to

2 o'clock is good); and where the pitching hand is when the stride foot lands (2 to 5 o'clock is good). These vary a little bit according to the pitch being thrown.

Speed drills: The distance throw (long toss) will increase speed. All the mechanics that produce speed will produce distance. The pitcher who can throw the fastest can also throw the furthest. All the mechanical problems which take away from speed will also take away from distance. It is a good practice for beginning and intermediate pitchers to long toss at least the length of a gym. The two drills that will help speed the most are (1) speed walking through the pitches to perfect timing and leg push, and (2) long toss which promotes the long lever, follow through and good posture.

Being able to relax the muscles instead of "muscling up" always allows greater arm speed and hand speed during the circle and release.

In summary about speed, faster motion and relaxed joint flexion produce faster ball speed. Application of power in one plane and in one direction produces faster ball speed. Timing the release and the forward motion together will produce faster ball speed. Release mechanics and timing that cause acceleration at the release will cause greater speed.

On the other side of the coin, bending forward at the waist, bending the landing knee, bending the elbow in the arm circle or during the release, rotating the arm on its long axis during the arm circle, stopping the arm at the release point, rotating on the pivot foot in the beginning of the circle, and landing with the stride foot while in the front half of the arm circle will all take away from the speed.

CHAPTER 3 – Control Issues

Control is the result of a combination of (1) the absence of injury and injury prone mechanics and training practices, (2) consistent practicing and repetitions performing mechanical form and using a consistent release point, and (3) knowledge of the problems that occur and problem-solving strategy for each one.

It is possible to have good control and poor mechanics if enough repetition takes place because practice makes permanent. The mechanics and practice habits used should be those that will cause both pitching success and a healthy athlete.

There are any number of training practices that can be hurtful to pitchers. I have watched various types of weight room exercises which should never have occurred.

A pitcher will benefit from workouts which will in general make her stronger overall and more cardiovascular fit. Beyond that, it is recommended that weight training be geared to high repetition, low resistance training, with emphasis on endurance, range of motion, flexibility, and quickness rather than maxing out. Exercises can be tailored to fit the needs of a softball pitcher and the muscles and joints used in pitching.

While softball and pitching have evolved a long way in the past thirty years, there are still people out there saying to throw 500 pitches a day or still teaching "slamming the door" shoulder and hip turns during the release. There are even some who have a pitcher swing a weighted bucket around the circle which is very dangerous to the shoulder and lower back. Various other mechanics such as crossing over to land with the stride step and twisting back with the shoulders to throw the curve are also potentially harmful teaching strategies still sometimes taught.

Posture on the Drop – Emily Page

Eliminate jerky starts and stops in the
pitching motion. A jerk at the beginning

tends to cause another one at the end. The smoother all the motion, the faster and more controlled the pitcher will be.

One further thing that has caused much trouble for pitchers is pitching "batting practice." There is a difference between batting practice and "pitching practice." Batting practice will require pitching after the muscles are too tired to perform correct mechanics and can change the muscle memory and the release points of her pitches.

"Control drill"

It is easy to set up a target practice and get high repetitions at hitting spots. A cement block wall or brick wall can have a strike zone painted on it with numbered zones. The pitcher starts at a shorter distance than real, and throws full speed, seeing how many times out of ten she can hit each area. The focus here is to take the mind off whether she can throw a strike and instead cause her to throw to a location. When the percentage of successful pitches is above 50%, she may move back to the real distance and do the

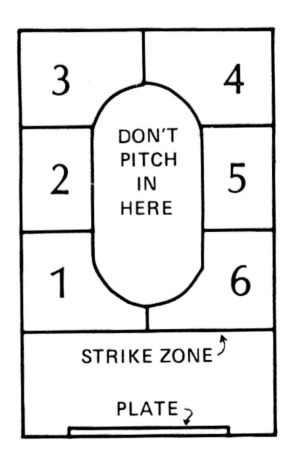

drill again. Upon reaching 50% this time, the drill changes to playing "around the world" hitting each number in sequence and seeing how many pitches it takes.

This drill works for beginning, intermediate, and also advanced pitchers by throwing their various pitches to their appropriate areas on the target.

The pitcher needs to establish and hold to a consistent warmup routine which will make everything the same every day. Going through the spins and posture and timing with arm swings, then full circle half speed, and finally full speed will be a help in making the release points permanent and knowing how to correct mistakes. This same routine done every day at the beginning of practice will then become the pitcher's warmup routine before starting a game. Keep in mind that the answer to fixing any pitch should not be changing the mechanics or throwing slower speed, but to use the mechanics of throwing fast until it is mastered.

There are so many reasons for being wild that it is impossible to name them all. Most of the time the correction to be given should be about what caused the wrong mechanics instead of about the mechanics. For example, a pitcher throws the drop low or into the ground because she is bending forward at the waist before releasing the ball. Rather than correcting the bending forward, its cause may be that she is picking up her back foot which makes her tilt forward at the release point. A hundred coaches have told her to stop bending forward, so if you say it too, she just stresses out. But you can correct it without mentioning the stress words by having her drag her back foot more forcefully. Corrections for control vary even with each pitch, so I am listing the location problem and telling the causes or corrections. Keep in mind that if more than two things are wrong, the corrections for any of them might not work until the other correction is made. The mistake and correction of each thing must be isolated and corrected. Often a pitcher cannot feel what is wrong. Muscle memory is built much better doing things slow motion with high repetitions, so that the pitcher recognizes the feeling of correct form.

"Control Errors and Corrections"

Wild low to pitching hand side:

(causes) Closing the pitching shoulder too early, no follow through, hips closed before release, crossing over the pivot foot in the back.

(corrections) Keeping the pitching side

shoulder still during the release, closing the shoulder late or after the release, dragging the pivot foot.

Wild high:

(causes) Releasing too late or too far out from the body. Too long a stride making the pitcher fall back. Landing with the stride foot turned 90 degrees also causes fallback. Bending at the waist before the ball is released makes the release late. Bending the elbow in the release lifts the release.

(corrections) Work on muscle memory of the release point - arm swing drills releasing spins to catcher, half-speed half-distance drills with full arm circle. Marking the landing spot on the ground for the pitches. Walking through all the pitch releases with two steps after the release.

Wild low:

(causes) Stopping the arm at the bottom of the circle, cocking the wrist back with the palm down near the release point, tilting posture forward during the release, bending forward at the waist during the release.

(corrections) Practicing the follow through. Walking through the pitches to maintain posture.

Wild to the sides:

(causes) Squashing the bug with the pivot foot or rotating the shoulders too far or rotating the pitching shoulder back in the top or top back of the circle. Closing the shoulders before the release or during the release. Coming up the front of the circle out to the side or away from the hip.

(corrections) If the pitcher is throwing to the pitching arm side, make the hand pass in front of the face in the front of the circle. That tilts the plane of the circle to the other side of the plate. Utilize a knee bend and push away with the pivot foot and leg to eliminate squashing the bug. Practicing the curve and screw in stride position tends to minimize the feet getting out of place and the shoulder turn and makes the pitcher rely on the hand position instead of the shoulder for location and spin.

Changeup high:

(cause) Leaving the back foot back. Taking too big a stride. Tilting posture back. Releasing with the palm up.

(corrections) Practice throwing it on a line at half the distance. Walk through the release.

Practice throwing it with the motion and posture and grips of the other pitches but with the changeup release.

Just as the player must practice in order to correct mistakes and make permanent good form, the pitching coach must work with many kids to see things wrong and recognize them quicker and learn how to correct them. Part of being a good pitching coach is getting the pitcher to stay calm and to understand pitching and the corrections. Learning to correct pitchers of different personalities is as much a skill as recognizing mechanical mistakes.

"Control Location to Batters"

Just as important as correcting mechanics, is knowing, throwing and controlling locations

For certain types of hitters. One concept of control for a pitcher, is the pitcher controlling or limiting where the batter can hit the ball. Here are some strategies for different types of hitters.

RHB forward in the box: Inside fast pitches, riseball, screwball and changeup.

LHB forward in the box: Inside fast pitches, riseball, screwball and changeup. Surprise with opposites sometimes.

RHB back in the box: Low pitches, drop, screw, curve. Riseball away or when ahead in the count.

LHB back in the box: Hard down and in, changeup away, rise and screw away.
RHB crowds the plate (likes it inside): Outside drop and rise, inside change and screw.

LHB crowds the plate (likes it inside): Hard down and in, drop, screw, rise away, change inside.

RHB away from the plate (likes it outside): Jam the batter inside with all pitches.

LHB away from the plate (likes it outside)
Jamb the batter inside with all pitches.

Contact hitter with speed: control where the batter hits the ball. With runners on base make the batter hit to the left side. Change speeds and try to cause off-balance contact or jamb in and fool away. This batter will take pitches, so must get ahead in the count.

Power hitter with big swing: Inside hard both up and down, and changeup; curve off the plate away. This batter does not like to walk, so will swing at pitcher's location pitches.

Batter dips or drops hands in the swing: Riseballs and high pitches and inside changeup.

Batter keeps hands up and chops at the ball: Drop, screw, and off-speed pitches.

Good bunter and sacrifice situations: Keep it inside to the RHB, up or down – trying to jam the batter or get a popup; away up and down to the LHB and change speeds – make them reach or wait so she can't start toward first while bunting.

With two strikes: Throw a "pitcher's pitch" out of the strike zone to any good hitter, either up, down, or away. Against a weak hitter do not waste pitches and strike her out on the next pitch.

With three balls: Her most reliable pitch, the one the pitcher is most confident in.

Bases loaded and high-pressure situations: Choose the pitcher's best pitch most of the time.

CHAPTER 4 – Ball Movement

In addition to the mechanics which produce ball speed and control, the things that produce the sharpest movement of the ball are (1) the axis and spin speed of the ball in its flight, (2) the leverage caused by body posture and stride length, (3) timing the release in relation to the pushing and landing feet, and (4) acceleration of the ball during flight toward the plate. These will cause the ball movement to be more dramatic and sudden.

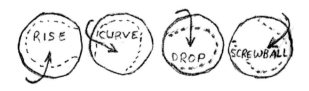

As the ball travels toward the plate, the front of the ball has resistance to the air. By the axis of its spin, some parts of the ball have less resistance, and the ball will curve in that direction.

The axis of ball spin needs to be perpendicular to the direction of the ball flight to get the maximum break and most sudden break. The greater the ratio of ball rotations to ball speed, the more a ball will break.

Body posture needs to give a mechanical advantage to the force applied to the ball. Force application producing the spin needs to be applied in a direction toward home plate. The best body posture needed for each pitch is accomplished by the stride length.

The release point timing for the rise, screw, and change is best when it's near the push of the back foot. The timing for the curve and drop are best when the release is near the landing of the front foot.

Acceleration of the ball in its flight toward the plate is accomplished by acceleration of the arm speed in the delivery through the release point and the application of a whipping action force in the release which is faster than the arm speed.

Riseball

The power riseball is the most dominant pitch in softball. After the batter must start her swing, the flight of the ball rises, making the bat-swing under the ball. The batter is even more vulnerable if there

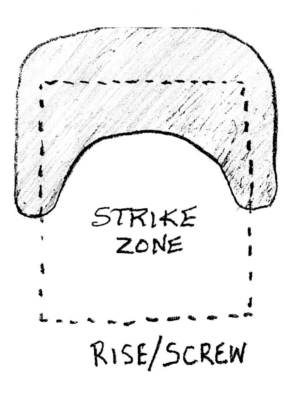

STRIKE ZONE

RISE/SCREW

are two strikes and she must swing at a good one. The rise is thrown at the top of the strike zone, and the batter must commit before the ball disappears upward. It is common for young pitchers to think the are throwing a riseball when they are throwing a fastball and the spin has not caught up with the speed. There are also many who can throw a ball that angles upward with corkscrew spin that is the result of a curve release wrist-snap. The ball will curve toward the point of the axis, so it rises.

Riseball – Coach Webb

However, the true rise has very tight straight back spin, and when it is thrown with power and acceleration, it changes directions suddenly and seems to jump upward. The later and more sudden the break, the less chance a batter has of hitting the ball. Because the ball must overcome gravity to rise, the faster the pitch is thrown (with correct spin) the more it will rise.

There are several common grips for the riseball. The simplest is to grip the ball like a fastball and then pull back the index finger so it is somewhat curled (not knuckled) and the inside corner of the nail is digging into the ball. The thumb should be opposite the ring finger on the ball and the end of the thumb have a very loose grip. During the release the index finger pushes through the ball.

The grip which will impart the fastest spin is difficult for anyone with small hands or short fingers. Lay the index finger down on its inside, slightly curled, like a circle-change grip. During the release, the ball rolls up the side of this finger.

There are many keys to the mechanics of the riseball. The posture and balance is upright, not leaning back or forward, and the stride is the longest of the movement pitches. The pushing foot is dominant for this pitch, and the push should come in the back half of the arm circle. In the front of the circle, the fingers point toward home, and in the back half of the circle the fingers point up (not out or back).

The elbow should stay straight past the bottom of the circle, flattening out the release point, and the palm should face out during the first half of the wrist snap, with the fingers cupped under the ball. If the elbow bends or the shoulder closes early or the wrist snap is across instead of out, then the palm will face forward at the release and the spin will be corkscrew. During the release the fingers close, little finger first, ring finger, middle finger, and index finger last, rolling the ball out of the hand in a slinging motion.

The follow through should be out then up, as though punching the opponent in the stomach, not the chin. The elbow should finish away from the ribs.

Screwball

The upward screwball is a form of the riseball. Pitchers lose some mechanical advantage on this pitch if they step too far to the side to accomplish an inside-out motion. The spin and movement need to come from the hand and not from the shoulder or posture. The stride should be two shoe widths to the side of the riseball stride and a half shoe length shorter. The arm is going to stay straight further into the follow through and the palm will face forward during the release, twisting the door knob and following through toward the thumb.

The spin axis of the ball will be tilted upward and to the pitching arm side of the plate, and the ball will tail toward the direction of the point of the spin axis. Stepping too far to the side or leaning to the side during the arm circle will cause the arm to come up beside the body instead of out in front and will lose the power of the legs.

The downward screwball can be accomplished several ways. The most common is to hold the ball with a drop or curve grip and accomplish the wrist snap sideways from behind the ball with the fingers pointed at the ground and the thumb forward. This wrist snap is behind or inside the ball, compared to the curve and drop which cause the hand to go over or under the ball during the release. This ball will have a true screw spin (opposite of the curve).

Curve – Lindsey Carnley

Curveball

The muscle memory similarities between the rise and curve will cause a pitcher who throws the curve too much to lose the riseball. The riseball is the more important pitch and is a power challenge pitch. The curve is a finesse or purpose pitch. The curve stays in more of a flat plane like the plane of the bat-swing, so a mistake over the plate will likely cause a bad result.

I recommend using the same grip as the rise, as it is a decoy that prevents the opposing players and coaches from recognizing it. The stride for the curve needs to be the shoe length less than the stride of the rise. The curve is thrown 90-95%, not full-speed. If thrown too hard, the curve will happen behind the plate instead of in front of the plate. The purpose of the curve is to get the batters to chase an outside pitch going away from them, or to jam the batters inside.

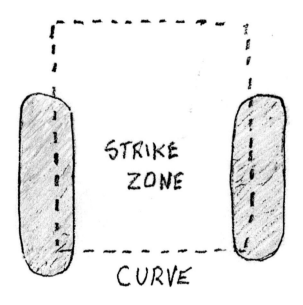

STRIKE
ZONE

CURVE

With the curve, the front foot is the dominant foot, and the balance of the release needs to be tall, and up over the front foot. Bending at the waist, leaving the pivot foot back, and leaning forward or back will cause the release to be away from the body and make the pitch high or away. The release and follow through should be close to the body.

The front ¾ of the arm circle is the same as the rise. In the lower back of the circle the hand becomes more cupped, with the hand turning sideways under the ball at the release and the little finger and ring finger squeezing the glove side of the ball as it is released. To learn or practice this spin, throw a pitching spinner flat like a Frisbee. The height of the curve can be caused by the location of the snap and follow through. Follow through to the front hip will be lower, and to the outside hip will be higher location.

Drop

While the riseball gets the most strikeouts and is the most dominant pitch, the drop keeps the ball in play, and is much less likely to walk batters.

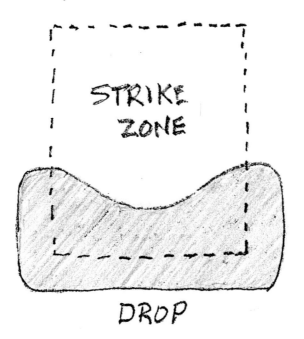

DROP

Drop – Holly Satterfield

The drop is easy for most pitchers to learn because the spin is usually the same as their fastball. The trick is to increase the spin speed without losing the ball speed.

In the next photo, Kelly is throwing a "peel drop" where the hand comes up the back side of the ball. When done correctly, this can cause a powerful and sudden drop. The problem is that many pitchers lift the ball during this release, and by throwing it harder also throw it higher in the strike zone. Then it becomes a HR pitch.

Another style often taught is the rollover drop. The palm is up in the lower back part of the circle, and the arm rotates inward on its long axis during the release and usually the follow through ends low with the thumb pointed down and pinkie up. The problems of this pitch are that it can cause shoulder problems to the rotator cuff, and that it loses speed from rotating the arm on its long axis.

What I recommend is called a "slap drop." It is gripped like a fastball so that it will spin with four seams. The release will be like the peel drop except the release force is slapped across the ball instead of up the back of the ball. The fingers close in the opposite order from the rise and curve - index finger first, then middle, then the ring finger and pinkie are the last to touch the ball as it is leaving the hand.

The stride is the same as the curve, a shoe length less than the rise, and the balance is tall over the dominant front foot. Leaning back will cause lifting the ball and will slow the spin. The pitcher will slightly bend forward at the waist just after the release point from having applied force forward and down. When the "slap" happens, it should cause the shoulders to push forward and all five fingers will end up pointing down. Unlike the peel drop, the harder this pitch is thrown, the lower it gets and the more break it has. It gets better as the pitcher tires, whereas the peel drop starts to hang up high as the pitcher tires.

The correct release for this is at the bottom of the arm circle, not out in front. The wrist snap is similar to a fastball, but a little later. The correct spin and location happen when the release is short.

Peel Drop – Kelly Zeilstra

Change/Off-speed

Backspin Change – Suzie McDonald

There are dozens of change-ups, so rather than teach a specific one, I want to talk about the change-up or off-speed pitch in general. There are three components to the change-up: (1) the mechanics which take away speed, (2) effective acting to fool the batter, and (3) the knowledge of when and where to throw it.

Palm Change – Holly Satterfield

One mechanical strategy which takes away speed is to shorten the lever. The ball comes from the middle of the hand instead of from the fingertips. A second mechanical strategy which takes away speed is to take away the wrist snap by keeping the wrist stiff and straight or by taking away the wrist leverage by flipping the ball backhand. Another method is to "give in" with the wrist at the release, causing a "negative" wrist snap. The control of the change-up is by the hand position in the release and by bringing the back foot up quickly.

Acting is by body language before and during the pitch. The arm-speed and style must be similar to faster pitches for the purpose of deception. The right time to throw the change is on counts that are effective (when the pitcher is ahead in the count, and any count when the batter does not suspect it). The change is more effective to an aggressive hitter. The most effective placement strategy is a location that is similar to the last pitch, or inside where a hitter can only pull it foul.

Remember the change also sets up the next pitch which should be something fast or inside to the batter. Coaches who are calling signals may want to keep a chart that shows the sequence of pitches each batter has been thrown and what and where the batter hit.

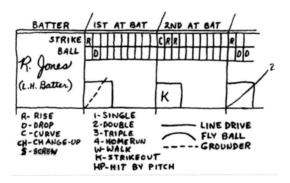

CHAPTER 5 - Coaches

Coaches are special people. They have a unique influence on people and on the future. They usually work for not so much money but can receive rewards that will last a lifetime. We all know some who have influenced us.

To be a good coach requires many things. Real authority must be earned, and kids are brutally honest about what is happening. They can see through someone who is not honest or not knowledgeable in a heartbeat.

You must be yourself, and yet you can never stop trying to be better.

Being a winner is more than the final score. It is about character, discipline, compassion and about work, sweat and pain and about life and love.

In this chapter I want to point out some coaches who were meaningful to me and some of the reasons. I hope those of you who are athletes will think of some of your coaches who have helped you become who you are today, and that you will want to become a coach one day too. To the coaches reading this, I just say thank you for the special work you do and don't forget the ones who opened the path for you.

To be a coach, one has to be an individual; but to be a good coach, the purpose of your life cannot be about yourself. It must be about the people around you, and how you can make them better.

John Bass had the politeness of a diplomat and southern gentleman. When he first came to me, it was because of his love for fast pitch softball. He had coached mostly boys, and had won several national and world

John Bass

titles coaching boys. John was a cheerful personality who could analyze what was wrong and what was right. He could teach with examples and explanations everyone could understand, and he could demonstrate. He got a special joy out of helping others.

John had been a professional roller skate dancer, and had a special balance and grace from that, and also an etiquette. He was humble, never putting others down, and open to hear other opinions and beliefs. He took care of his mother as long as she lived, and he collected coins, and worked at the post office for many years. He was respected by all who knew him. If he had an enemy, I don't know who it would have been. John volunteered to help me. He didn't ask for a cap or a uniform or to have his photo in the team picture. He didn't receive any money for being an assistant. He just wanted to help, and he wanted to promote good pitching and for us to win as a result of it.

To me, John is an example of "if you want to be good at something, start by being a good person." Second, learn all you can about what you are doing, and never stop learning...important lessons for coaching. Thank you, John.

Dave Swisegood

Dave coached baseball and basketball. In fact, in the sport of high school baseball, he holds the record for most total games won. My association with Dave was that he was a teammate for many years on the summer softball teams where I played; and secondly, the majority of teammates I had during twenty plus years had played high school baseball or basketball for him. Not that many people I know can coach kids and then be a competitor with them and maintain their professional respect. Dave was one who could and did. All the people I participated with still treated him as their coach, and he teased them and reminded them of all the things they had done and not done for the past twenty or thirty years. Everyone knew him for miles around. He coached kids who were the grandchildren of the first kids he coached. His enthusiasm and inner youth never stopped. I never really knew how old Dave was, but I was pretty sure that he was playing very competitive softball in his sixties and still teaching kids how to hustle, how to talk, how to play, how to think, and even how to make mistakes and recover from them. I remember one time he got in a rundown and, of course, he knew he would be out. He turned to the umpire before he could be tagged and yelled, "Time out!" Even the members of the other teams liked him. He could make the game fun and get everyone to relax. We played in a tournament one time, and there were two older fans that I appointed to choose an all-tournament team. When the tournament was over, and he hadn't gotten even one hit, the two fans announced the team, and they announced him at first base. Later I asked them why, and they just shrugged and said no one could hold a candle to Dave.

A coach should model what they teach, they must love what they do, and they must teach others to love what they do. These are what Dave did and what he is still doing. An awesome coach! Thank you, Dave.

Jean Williams

My coaching was truly blessed to know this lady. Those of you who know women's athletics and its history understand that some major battles had to be fought in the early days, and Jean did this. She became one of the foremost athletic directors in the NJCAA and in rules interpretations and judgments. She coached most of her career in slowpitch softball, and when she retired from that, she was my volunteer assistant for fastpitch. Her dedication and the respect for her that I saw from presidents and administrators of colleges and from former players is unequalled. She was a leader.

In my job interview, when the state of Florida was switching over from slowpitch to fastpitch, and she was retiring from having won 17 consecutive conference championships and 7 national championships, she asked me this question. "Jim, what is your philosophy on defense?" My answer was "to strike out 21 batters." But over the next few years, I learned many defensive lessons from Jean. Defense wins championships. I still use drills today that I learned from her.

Not too long after that I attended Jean's retirement banquet. There were speakers there from many places, and many former players who told stories about their most loved coach. It was an experience I'll never forget, and an inspiration to me ever since. That night they read a handful of letters, congratulating her on her career and her retirement. They read letters from several college presidents, they read one from the mayor of the town, they read some from her former players, and they read some from other athletic directors and from the state athletic association. When they were down to only a couple left, the next one was from the governor of the state of Florida, and I thought who could the next one be? Well, the next one was from the President of the United States. Then someone who was thinking the same as me said out loud "Who's the last one from, God?" It almost was, as Jean, being a full-blooded Florida State fan, the last one was from Bobby Bowden, the Florida State football coach.

Jean is one of the few coaches I have known who hated losing as much as I did. She took care of her own house at Lake City CC, winning championship after championship, and turning out young ladies who were inspired to follow in her footsteps. And at the same time, she was a national influence for girl's participation, scholarships and opportunities for women in sports. I don't know anyone who has done more, or who has been more knowledgeable or more principled.

On a personal note, she was a friend, and someone I admire for her wisdom, understanding, and commitment. There doesn't seem to be many coaches who will take the high road to get where they want to go. The point: don't take short cuts. Do what is right, and do what you believe in. Make

Your priorities about people and rules and about understanding both.

I want to state part of a quote that I heard Jean give a number of times. I am giving the beginning and the ending – please look up the middle on the internet and read it all:

"Class never runs scared. It is sure-footed and confident, and it can handle whatever comes along… If you have class, you've got it made. If you don't have class, no matter what else you have, it won't make up for it." Coach and teach with class. Jean did. Thank you, Jean.

"Others and More"

I would like you to think of some of the coaches you know who have made a difference in your life. Put them in your own "Hall of Fame" and then you strive to join them there. Being good is more than about pitching and more than about softball and more than about sports. Being your best at whatever you do will make the world around you a better place and inspire others to do the same.

A word of advice to young or new coaches: Seek out the most successful coaches in your area and

Become friends with them. Talk to them, ask them questions, watch how they do things, take note of what causes their success. Watch them and listen to them in practice and in games. Study what it is about them that causes the impact they have. These are living lessons that will help you.

Vince Lombardi said it this way: "The quality of a person's life is in direct proportion to their commitment to excellence, regardless of their chosen field of endeavor."

CHAPTER 6 – Believe in Miracles

When I was young, I believed I would do miracles; when I was older, I got to be part of quite a few miracles and got to witness a lot of miracles; and now I believe that I can teach and coach miracles. Teaching is the most fun when the students learn to believe in themselves. The person who believes in miracles does have the ability to make them happen.

When opportunity and preparation meet, there is success. Everyone wants to win, but not everyone wants to prepare. For those who prepare, the opportunity will come. Failing to prepare is preparing to fail. The miracles that I have been part of involve ordinary people who did extraordinary things. They began as ordinary people, but they did not behave like ordinary people and they did not stay ordinary. That is why you and I have a chance to become a miracle.

In this chapter I will tell a shortened version of a number of miracles. They all involve preparation meeting opportunity. They all involve the process of ordinary people becoming extraordinary. I was part of the process in many of the cases, but I was not necessarily the cause. The cause is something inside a person where there is a fire or passion to be better than others believe or expect. Sometimes believing in someone was enough to bring it out. Sometimes playing catch for thousands of hours caused it. Sometimes this person just willed herself to win and refused to accept defeat. I am listing them in a chronological order they happened, not the order of importance or size of the miracle or achievement.

Becky Duffin

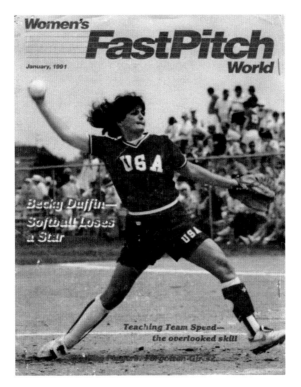

I was in my first year as a college head coach when I met Becky, and she was a college senior and our starting center fielder. She was a very good athlete, and one of our better players, but had never won any big honors. By appearance she was an ordinary young lady. When she learned to pitch, all that changed. In November that year, she began pitching and we sometimes played catch for 2 hours a day, and she would come find me on Saturday or Sunday evening to do more. Her first game was a shutout, and she ended that year second in the nation in strikeouts in NCAA division I. She went on to be an All-American in women's major competition, set many records, (62 strikeouts in a 33-inning game, walking only 2 and allowing only 2 hits). In a five-year career in women's major competition, she had 80 no-hitters. One summer alone she had 9 perfect games. Becky pitched the USA to the World Games championship in 1990. Her photo here was taken during those games and was the cover for the Women's Fastpitch World magazine after her death from cancer later that year.

Brenda Heyl

Brenda had an average freshman year at Western Illinois University, a team that finished near the bottom of the Gateway Conference. I joined the team as a pitching coach and helped Brenda develop a riseball and other pitches. Many hours of

Practice helped her lead the WIU team to win the conference tournament that year, and Brenda went on to break many of the school's pitching records and be placed in the WIU Sports Hall of Fame and her number retired. She completed her M.S. degree while being an assistant coach at WIU

Heather Schlichtman

Heather was in the 7th grade when she first came to me for pitching lessons. She kept getting better and better and kept growing taller and taller, reaching more than 6,,2". She learned a tremendous riseball and while still in high school was clocked at 67 mph. Her summer team, the Orange Park Storm, won the 16U- NSA nationals, and in her senior year of high school she did not allow a run the entire season. She played in college at the University of Arkansas.

Lisa McNeley

Lisa impressed me as a winner in the first few moments I met her. She spent a year learning the riseball with me at Lincoln College, and when I took the position as head coach at Lake City Community College in Florida, she asked to come along. In her sophomore season, Lisa led the nation in pitching wins and strikeouts; and in hitting HRs and RBIs while batting cleanup for the Timberwolves. She was named an All-American twice and finished her softball career at Florida Southern College.

Rachel Riddell

Rachel was another winner who played first

base and batted third in the lineup for Lake City. Riddell and McNeley were a fearsome combination. Rachel had a wicked flip change and a fastball that ran to either side. Once when McNeley had her tonsils out and could not play, Rachel pitched a double-header shutout with one of the games being a no-hitter. An intense competitor, she hated to lose, and it showed in her final won-loss record (22-1). Rachel was one of the best fielding pitchers I have ever coached. She was an All-American and went on from Lake City to play at Jacksonville State University.

Sara Pacheco

Sara came to Lake City CC from high altitude in the Colorado mountains, where the riseball does not work so well. When she learned it and led the region in strikeouts, she became a surprising force. She was part of another dynamic duo with TeRay Warneke, and usually pitched the second game of double-headers. It looked like she might have an undefeated season, but her only loss of the year came in the 1997 national championship game, and she finished the year at 28-1. Both she and TeRay were named All-American.

1997 Lady Timberwolves

To get out of regionals that year, Palm Beach CC with Crystal Bustos stood in the way. They were defending national champions and ranked #1 in the nation the whole year. We did not play them during the regular season so they would not see our pitchers, but the week before the regional tournament, in a team meeting, one of our players, Michelle Hildebrand, told a dream she had. We would meet PBCC in the championship game and would be down 1-0 in the bottom of the 7th, and she told who would bat, and how it would end. Every detail of the dream came true exactly as she told us, with Michelle herself getting the game winning hit to knock PBCC out of the 1997 playoffs. This "miracle" team finished second at nationals and had four players named All-American.

Jill Cecil

When I first played catch with Jill, she was the wildest pitcher I had ever worked with. Early in H.S. she broke the Iowa state record for walks in a game. However, she did not give up or quit and by her senior season, she led the state of Iowa in strikeouts. She continued her college career pitching for Coe College.

Jill Cecil

Kelly Zeilstra

I have not seen many players with the dedication and pure determination to excel that characterized Kelly. She came to Lake City CC to develop and reach her goals of playing on a top D-I team and then for Canada on their national team. During the 1998 season, with a 38-4 record, Kelly led the Lady Wolves to a #1 ranking in the nation the entire season and was named a first team All-American. She went on to play two years at Big Ten conference champion Iowa, lead the Big Ten in ERA, and played for the Canada national team for six years.

Michelle Rowe

On the surface Michelle seemed an average pitcher, but I recruited her because of her intensity and because she refused to lose. Her top speed was probably 55 mph, but she had good movement and pinpoint control.

She became a first-team All-American (28-3 record) as a college freshman and had wins over the top 5 finishers at the NJCAA nationals. In the fall of 1999, she had wins over both Florida State (3-0 shutout) and Florida (3-1 four hitter).

Jessica Leenerts

On my first day at Culver-Stockton College, my assistant, Ed Heller, introduced me to his prize local freshman recruit, Jessica Leenerts. We played catch, and I told her that day she could break all the pitching records at CSC. She learned the riseball, and we won regionals and made the school's first ever trip to the NAIA nationals. Jessica broke the school career strikeout record in a single season. She was national player of the week twice on her way to being named an NAIA All-American as a freshman.

Natalia Morozova

I first met and worked with Natasha when she was 10 and playing shortstop (left-handed) for the 10U Russian girls team. At the age of 12 she led them to the European Little League championship and took them to Kirkland, Washington for the Little League World Series. Since then she also won the European Pony championship and played on scholarship at Darton College where she was named an NJCAA All-American, and then at Valdosta State University, winning an NCAA division II national championship.

"Believing in Yourself"

Can you be a miracle? Of course you can. With hard work, dedication, and preparation, you can be ready when opportunity knocks at the door.

The purpose of this book is to give you the information that can help you become a miracle.

CHAPTER 7 – Summary

My hope is that this book is useful for coaches and for all athletes from beginning to advanced skill level. It is meant to help you recognize problems and make corrections. Many of the technical parts of the book concern making little adjustments, but these little things can be the difference between being poor or average, or the difference between being average and good, or the difference between being good and great. For sure, many times they will be the difference between winning and losing.

The most important factor in becoming a good pitcher is "how much you want it," and that is measured by how hard you work and how persistent and dedicated you are to excellence and class.

Speed is caused by a fast arm circle in one plane which passes through the strike zone; by a relaxed wrist snap from the fingertips; by the longest lever possible during the release; and in a tall and balanced, powerful body position; and is timed with the leg drive to get the most force from the large muscles of the legs.

Control is the process of performing high repetitions as smoothly as possible and knowing and using the corrections for location mistakes.

Learning the movement pitches depends on the ability to maintain proper body position to impart the proper spin and location to the ball. The posture, balance, timing, and dominant foot during the release are as important as the grip on the ball.

The instruction to have speed or control is not complicated, and these things apply equally to the pitchers of all ages, sizes, and experience levels.

The correct order of learning is: learn a smooth delivery to be able to reasonably control throwing your fastest speed; then learn a changeup; then learn movement pitches. If done in this order, a pitcher may begin the movement pitches at any age or size. In learning movement pitches, the rise should be learned first and made permanent before learning the curve.

Coaching and teaching is very important. The lessons that I learned from the coaches who influenced me were to be a good person, never stop learning or teaching, impart my love of the game and knowledge of skills to my students, and be professional with respect for the game, its rules, and all its participants.

Challenges:

To the pitchers, as you mature in your knowledge and ability, it is my advice for you to take some younger players and teach them. It will take you to a new level in your own performance.

To the coaches, thank you for coaching, for caring about kids, for your love of the game of fastpitch, and for continuing to learn. Set a goal that is higher than winning games, set a goal that you will pass on what you know and feel so it will cause your players to want to coach someday.

To everyone who reads this: Appreciate your coaches (or players) and thank them. Appreciate your parents and thank them. Appreciate your teammates and thank them. Appreciate the umpires and thank them. Maybe one day you will be a coach. Maybe one day you will be a parent. Maybe one day you will be an umpire. One thing is for sure, if you work at this, you will have an impact on people around you and on your future. Do not settle for being ordinary. Be special.

"Care more than others think is wise. Risk more than others think is safe. Dream more than others think is practical. Expect more than others think is possible."

Prove that YOU "Believe in Miracles." Be one yourself.

You can be at the end of the Rainbow

Made in the USA
Las Vegas, NV
25 January 2021